My

Cat

by Hayley Lee
illustrations by Ethan Long

Harcourt Brace & Company

Orlando Atlanta Austin Boston San Francisco Chicago Dallas New York Toronto London

My cat is Tab.

Tab will tap on a mat.

Tab will tap on a can.

Tab will tap on a pan.

Tab will tap on my lap.

Tab will tap on
my hat.

Tab will not nap.

Tab will TAP!